THE IRAQ WAR
12 THINGS TO KNOW

by Jon Westmark

www.12StoryLibrary.com

12-Story Library is an imprint of Peterson Publishing Company and Press Room Editions.

Produced for 12-Story Library by Red Line Editorial

Photographs ©: Staff Sgt. Stacy L. Pearsall/US Air Force, cover, 1; AP Images, 4, 22; Laurent Rebours/AP Images, 5; Chao Soi Cheong/AP Images, 6, 28; davidevison/iStockphoto, 7; Reuters/Corbis, 8; Staff Sgt. Michael D. Gaddis/US Air Force, 9; Hussein Malla/AP Images, 10; J. Scott Applewhite/AP Images, 11; Photographer's Mate 1st Class Arlo K. Abrahamson/US Navy, 12; Wally Santana/AP Images, 13; Public Domain, 14; Evan Vucci/AP Images, 15; Cpl. Trevor Gift/US Marine Corps, 16; Lance Cpl. Sheila M. Brooks/US Marine Corps, 17; US Department of Defense, 18, 19; Khalid Mohammed/AP Images, 20; US Department of Defense/American Forces Information Service/Defense Visual Information Center, 21; James (Jim) Gordon CC2.0, 23; Wathiq Khuzaie/AP Images, 24; Maya Alleruzzo/AP Images, 25, 29; William Abenhaim/SIPA/1511140937/AP Images, 27

Content Consultant: Dr. Lisa Leitz, PhD in Sociology, Assistant Professor in Peace Studies and Sociology, Chapman University

Library of Congress Cataloging-in-Publication Data
Names: Westmark, Jon, 1990- author.
Title: The Iraq War : 12 things to know / by Jon Westmark.
Other titles: Iraq War, twelve things to know
Description: Mankato, MN : 12-Story Library, [2017] | Series: America at war
    | Includes bibliographical references and index. | Audience: Grades 4-6.
Identifiers: LCCN 2016002424 (print) | LCCN 2016002586 (ebook) | ISBN
    9781632352668 (library bound : alk. paper) | ISBN 9781632353160 (pbk. :
    alk. paper) | ISBN 9781621434351 (hosted ebook)
Subjects: LCSH: Iraq War, 2003-2011--Juvenile literature.
Classification: LCC DS79.763 .W47 2016 (print) | LCC DS79.763 (ebook) | DDC
    956.7044/3--dc23
LC record available at http://lccn.loc.gov/2016002424

Printed in the United States of America
Mankato, MN
May, 2016

Access free, up-to-date content on this topic plus a full digital version of this book. Scan the QR code on page 31 or use your school's login at 12StoryLibrary.com.

Table of Contents

1

Operation Desert Storm Pushes Hussein Back

Tensions were high in the Middle East in the summer of 1990. The leader of Iraq was Saddam Hussein. He was upset with the country of Kuwait. It was producing too much oil and Hussein claimed it was stealing oil from Iraq. This drove down the price of oil. Iraq's economy largely depends on oil sales. The lower rates hurt Iraq's economy. On August 2, 1990, Hussein sent Iraqi forces into Kuwait. The small country quickly fell under Iraqi control.

Kuwait's government asked for international support. The United States and a number of other nations responded. They sent troops to the region. The conflict became known as the Persian Gulf War. The first part of the war was called Operation Desert Shield. Troops built up and prepared

for combat. On January 17, 1991, the next stage of the war began. It was called Operation Desert Storm and had the support of the United Nations (UN). For more than a month, US air strikes bombarded Iraqi forces. US-led ground forces moved in on February 24. On February 28, US President George H. W. Bush said Kuwait was free. He declared an end to the fighting.

Hussein's troops were forced to retreat from Kuwait.

Saddam Hussein became president of Iraq on July 16, 1979.

4

But Hussein kept control of Iraq. In March 1991, groups of Iraqis rebelled against Hussein's government. Hussein used force to put down the uprisings. He remained in power. The UN worried about Hussein's use of force against Iraqis. It told Iraq to destroy all of its weapons of mass destruction. But in the mid-1990s, the UN got word Iraq may have been hiding many banned weapons. In response, in 1998, US president Bill Clinton decided to bomb the buildings where the weapons were said to be stored. Iraq began to cooperate less with UN weapons inspectors because there were US spies among them. Hussein's plans became even more of a mystery. An uneasy calm formed between the United States and Iraq.

100
Hours it took ground forces to free Kuwait from Iraqi control.

- Iraq invaded Kuwait on August 2, 1990.
- US-led air and ground strikes freed Kuwait by February 28, 1991.
- Saddam Hussein kept power in Iraq after the war.
- In April 1991, Hussein was ordered to destroy certain weapons.
- In 1998, the United States bombed Iraq after the UN found weapons there.

A helicopter herds Iraqi prisoners during Operation Desert Storm.

September 11 Attacks Shake the United States

On September 11, 2001, the United States faced a threat other than Saddam Hussein. At 8:46 a.m., disaster struck the World Trade Center in New York City. An airplane crashed into the side of the North Tower. Televisions across the United States showed live video of the aftermath. Smoke and flames spewed into the blue sky over New York's skyline. Rescue workers rushed to the scene. People were filled with questions. Had the crash been an accident? Had the pilot lost control of the airplane?

At 9:03 a.m. on September 11, 2001, United Airlines flight 175 crashed into the World Trade Center's South Tower.

The hijackers' second Washington, DC, target is thought to have been the White House or Capitol Building.

These questions were answered moments later. As people around the world watched, a second plane slammed into the South Tower. It became clear the crashes were not accidents. The airplanes had been hijacked. They were being used as weapons.

Two more airplanes were hijacked that morning. One took off from Washington, DC. It crashed nearby into the Pentagon. This is the headquarters of the US Department of Defense. The other plane took off from New Jersey. But it never made it to its target. People aboard the plane fought with the hijackers. The plane crashed into a field in Pennsylvania.

Both of the World Trade Center towers collapsed within two hours of being struck. Nearly 3,000 people died in the four attacks.

US President George W. Bush addressed the nation that evening. He assured Americans the search was underway for the terrorists responsible for the attacks.

403
Number of firefighters, police, and paramedics killed in the attacks on the World Trade Center.

- Hijackers took control of four airplanes.
- Two planes were crashed into the World Trade Center and one into the Pentagon.
- Passengers fought hijackers on the fourth plane, causing it to crash into a field.
- President George W. Bush promised to find the people responsible.

United States Declares War on Terror

On September 14, 2001, the US Congress passed a bill on terrorism. It allowed the United States to use force against the people responsible for the September 11 attacks. President Bush signed the bill on September 18.

On September 20, Bush announced the beginning of the War on Terror. The war's main target was al-Qaeda. This group planned and carried out the September 11 attacks. Al-Qaeda is a terrorist group. It follows a violent form of Islam that most Muslims reject. A Saudi man named Osama bin Laden led the group.

Bush said the first site of the War on Terror would be Afghanistan. A group called the Taliban ran the country. The Taliban was not a terrorist organization. But it enforced harsh laws and punished crimes in cruel ways. And it allowed al-Qaeda to operate in Afghanistan. The United States hoped to remove the Taliban from power. Doing so would make it harder for terrorist groups, such as al-Qaeda, to operate.

On October 7, the United States began Operation Enduring Freedom. US-led forces started bombing the Taliban in Afghanistan.

Bush said the war was not against another country. It was against terrorists around the world.

8

Ground troops moved in 12 days later. The Taliban fled from Afghanistan's capital, Kabul, in November. In December, they fled their stronghold, the southern city of Kandahar. Then, they went into the Afghan countryside and Pakistan. In February 2002, the UN helped Afghanistan start a new government.

A US Navy Tomcat prepares for a bombing mission in Afghanistan during Operation Enduring Freedom.

80

Percentage of Americans who supported sending troops to Afghanistan.

- On September 14, 2001, the US Congress passed a bill allowing use of force against terrorists.
- President Bush announced the War on Terror on September 20.
- US troops invaded Afghanistan on October 7 and began attacking the Taliban.
- In November, the Taliban fled Afghanistan's capital, Kabul. They fled their stronghold, Kandahar, in December.

OSAMA BIN LADEN

Osama bin Laden believed that Muslims should take part in a jihad, or struggle. For most Muslims, jihad is a peaceful struggle to be better followers of Islam. But bin Laden took an extreme view. He started al-Qaeda in 1988. The group became known for committing violent acts against non-Islamic countries, such as the United States. They thought of these attacks as a violent jihad. Bin Laden went into hiding after the September 11 attacks to protect himself. US troops found and killed him in Pakistan in May 2011.

US-Led Forces Oust Saddam Hussein

The Taliban was on the run. And a new government was in place in Afghanistan. The focus of the War on Terror shifted to Iraq. The US government believed Iraq leader Saddam Hussein gave al-Qaeda weapons, money, and training. And there was still concern Hussein was making weapons of mass destruction in Iraq. It thought he might use them against the coalition countries. The UN made threats against Hussein so he would let inspectors into the country. In November 2002, Hussein agreed to let them in. They did not find any weapons of mass destruction. But the leaders of the United States and Great Britain did not believe it.

The US Congress passed a bill in October 2002. It let the United States use force in Iraq. The UN did not approve. But the United States formed a coalition with other countries that supported going to war. On March 17, 2003, Bush demanded Hussein leave Iraq within 48 hours. Hussein refused.

From 1998 to November 2002, weapons inspectors were not allowed into Iraq to look for weapons of mass destruction.

49

Number of countries in the US-led coalition in March 2003.

- The US government worried Hussein had weapons of mass destruction and supported al-Qaeda.
- The United States formed a group of countries to invade Iraq.
- In the spring of 2003, US-led air and ground attacks drove Hussein's government out of Iraq.

AL-QAEDA IN IRAQ

In February 2003, US Secretary of State Colin Powell spoke to the UN. He made a case for going to war in Iraq. Powell said Hussein was connected to a man named Abu Musab al-Zarqawi. Zarqawi led groups that were connected to al-Qaeda. The 9/11 Commission later found no link between the two men. But Powell's speech helped Zarqawi gain influence in Iraq. In 2004, Zarqawi started a new group that the United States called al-Qaeda in Iraq (AQI).

On March 19, the Iraq War began. US-led forces began a massive bombing of the country. By mid-April, US-led forces controlled Iraq's biggest cities. This included Baghdad and Mosul. Hussein and his supporters had gone into hiding.

On May 1, 2003, Bush announced an end to operations in Iraq. But the war was far from over. Hussein's supporters were scattered. They continued to attack US-led forces.

Bush's May 1, 2003, speech took place on an aircraft carrier off the coast of San Diego, California.

5

Prisoner Treatment Draws Backlash

As fighting continued in Iraq, US troops hoped to get information that could prevent insurgent attacks. Insurgents led uprisings against the coalition. They did not want to be led by a foreign nation.

In addition to stopping attacks, US troops hoped to track down wanted people, such as Hussein. The United States gathered information from Iraqi prisoners. Some of the prisoners were common criminals. Others were terrorists. Some were innocent of any wrongdoing. Many were kept at Abu Ghraib prison, near Baghdad.

US troops helped secure Iraq from insurgent attacks.

On April 28, 2004, photos from inside Abu Ghraib prison were shown on American television. They showed inmates being abused and humiliated by US troops in charge of the prison. The photos caused an outcry around the world. People said the abuse went against the Geneva Conventions. Many countries, including the United States and Iraq, agreed to uphold these laws after World War II (1939–1945). The laws define the basic rights of wounded soldiers, civilians, and prisoners of war. But the US government said the laws did not protect terrorists.

The US Army investigated the treatment of prisoners at Abu Ghraib. They found that a number of US personnel had taken part in prisoner abuse. Eleven soldiers and officers who worked at and oversaw the prison were disciplined for their actions.

The abuses at Abu Ghraib hurt the United States' image around the world. One of the United States' goals in Iraq was to free Iraqis from oppression. The photos made people question if the United States respected the Iraqi people.

Framework of gates securing the main entrance of Abu Ghraib prison

212
Number of Abu Ghraib prisoners who filed charges of abuse.

- The United States held criminals, suspected terrorists, prisoners of war, and innocent people at Abu Ghraib prison.
- Photos from the prison showed abuse of prisoners.
- The photos caused many people to question what was actually going on in Iraq.

Bush Redefines Purpose of the Iraq War

In July 2004, the 9/11 Commission gave a report to the US Congress. Congress and President George W. Bush created the commission in

THE

9/11

COMMISSION REPORT

FINAL REPORT OF THE NATIONAL COMMISSION ON TERRORIST ATTACKS UPON THE UNITED STATES

2002. It was made up of members from different political parties. Its purpose was to report on US security weaknesses prior to September 11. The goal was to help prevent future attacks. In its report, the commission said it had not found any proof Hussein was working with al-Qaeda.

On October 6, 2004, the Iraq Survey Group (ISG) released a report. The ISG was a group of weapons experts. It was created by the coalition. Its job was to find weapons of mass destruction in Iraq. After more than 18 months of searching, it presented a 1,500-page report. The report said the United States did not have proof of weapons of mass destruction when it went to war with Iraq. US soldiers later found chemical

The 9/11 Commission's report can be found in bookstores across the United States.

THINK ABOUT IT

Do you think the United States should have waited to find more evidence before invading Iraq? Why?

0

Number of weapons of mass destruction found in Iraq before the Iraq War.

- In July 2004, the 9/11 Commission found no links between Hussein and al-Qaeda.
- Two months later, the Iraq Survey Group reported the United States went to war without proof of weapons of mass destruction in Iraq.
- Bush said the new purpose of the war was to bring democracy to Iraq.

weapons in Iraq. But the weapons were old and rusted. All had been built before 1991 with materials that were mostly from the United States and Great Britain.

Bush shifted the focus of the war from weapons of mass destruction and al-Qaeda. Instead, he said removing Saddam Hussein from power was the right thing to do. Hussein had been a brutal leader. He had executed anyone who opposed him. He had even attempted to kill off or remove all Kurdish people from Iraq. Bush said the coalition could now focus on setting up a democracy in Iraq.

Iraq Survey Group members speaking to the Senate Armed Services committee on October 6, 2004

Iraqis Hold First Elections in 50 Years

Hussein's government was gone. Iraqis needed new leadership. They had not been allowed to select their leaders when Hussein ruled the country. On January 30, 2005, they voted to select a national assembly. Its members would plan how the new government would work. The election was Iraq's first democratic vote since 1953. On election day, groups opposed to the democratic government assaulted voters across the country. But coalition troops patrolled cities. They helped keep most Iraqis safe while voting.

A large minority of the population, the Sunnis, boycotted the vote. Many Sunnis did not believe the new government would help fix Iraq's problems. Because of the boycott, the Sunnis were not well represented in the government.

National assembly representatives wrote a constitution. They also selected a president and prime minister. On October 15, 2005, Iraq's new constitution was approved. Sunnis thought it was unfair. They tried to change the

A total of 8 million Iraqis turned out to vote on January 30, 2005.

On December 15, 2005, people waited in line to vote in the mostly Sunni city of Husaybah, Iraq.

terms with a referendum. But it did not get enough votes to pass.

On December 15, 2005, Iraqis elected a parliament. This time, Sunnis turned out in large numbers to vote. They received much more representation in the government. Still, many Sunnis believed Prime Minister Nouri al-Maliki favored his own group, the Shiites.

15,000

Number of US soldiers who patrolled Baghdad during the January 2005 elections.

- Iraqis elected a national assembly on January 30, 2005.
- The representatives created a constitution, which was approved in October 2005.
- Iraqis elected a parliament in December 2005.
- Many Sunnis believed they were not well represented in the new government.

GROUPS IN IRAQ

Two of the main groups in Iraq are Sunnis and Shiites. Both groups are Arab, and they follow different versions of Islam. Approximately 60 percent of Iraqis are Shiites. Sunnis make up approximately 20 percent. The third main group in Iraq is the Kurds, who also make up approximately 20 percent of the population. Kurds may follow Sunni or Shiite versions of Islam, but they have their own language and culture. People of other faiths, such as Christians, and people who do not practice any faith make up only approximately 1 percent of the population.

17

8

New Technologies Help Keep Soldiers Safe

Iraq had a new leader and a more balanced government. But violence continued. The United States and coalition troops remained in the country to help the Iraqi government develop. Insurgent groups, such as AQI, fought against the new government and coalition troops. Members of these groups would attack suddenly and without warning.

The biggest threats to coalition troops in Iraq were improvised explosive devices (IEDs). Many troops were killed or wounded by IED attacks. These crude bombs could be hidden near roads where troops traveled. The US military found many ways to defend against IED attacks. One way was to stop the bombs from being planted.

Ammunition for an IED found in Iraq

THINK ABOUT IT

THINK ABOUT IT

What is the benefit of using a flying drone to watch over an area? What are the alternatives?

$50 billion

Amount spent on MRAPs during the Iraq War and the War in Afghanistan.

- Insurgents often placed IEDs near roads to attack US troops.
- Drones helped prevent IEDs from being deployed.
- MRAPs protected soldiers during IED explosions.

Drones helped with this effort. From the air, they watched roads. They looked for unusual activity. Drones gathered information without putting troops at risk of being hurt. But IEDs still posed a threat to many troops. Drones could not watch all parts of Iraq or stop all attacks.

Mine-Resistant Ambush-Protected (MRAP) vehicles helped keep troops safe from IEDs. These blast-proof trucks have V-shaped hulls. The shape helps deflect explosions from underneath the trucks to the sides of the trucks and away from them. This helps protect people riding in the vehicles. Some MRAPs have long robotic arms to handle IEDs. Others contain radio jammers. Jammers block devices from communicating with the IEDs. Doing so keeps IEDs from detonating. MRAPs helped protect soldiers. But they were expensive to make. Each MRAP cost approximately $1 million.

MRAPs helped decrease deaths and injuries from IEDs by 30 percent between 2000 and 2010.

Fighting Takes Toll on Iraqi Civilians

In 2006, fighting in Iraq ramped up. On February 22, members of al-Qaeda in Iraq (AQI) bombed a Shiite mosque in the city of Samarra. The building was a holy place for Shiites. AQI hoped the attack would start a civil war. It succeeded. A wave of violence broke out between Sunnis and Shiites. The coalition and Iraqi government tried to end the civil war by force. But violence increased. The fighting had a major effect on Iraqi citizens.

Most Iraqis were not involved in the fighting. But they were affected by the constant violence in their towns and cities. Many Iraqis were forced to leave their homes because of the dangerous conditions. Others had to leave because the coalition fighting had destroyed their communities. By the start of 2008, 4.7 million Iraqis were displaced. Some moved within the country. Many fled to other countries. They mainly went to nearby Syria and Jordan.

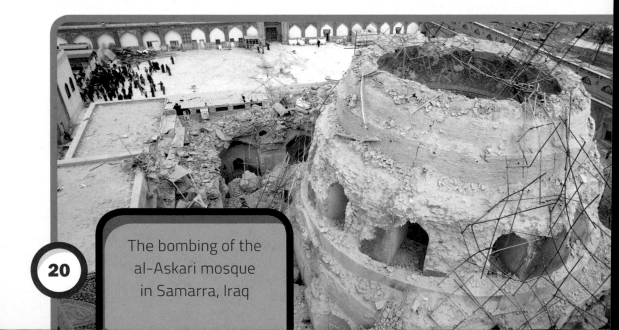

The bombing of the al-Askari mosque in Samarra, Iraq

2

Millions of Iraqis who fled to other nations.

- A civil war between Sunnis and Shiites broke out in 2006.
- The increased violence led many Iraqis to leave their homes.
- Iraqi refugees faced poor living conditions, diseases, and prejudice.

THINK ABOUT IT

Imagine you are forced to leave your home and go to a new place. What would that be like for you and your family?

Displaced Iraqis faced other problems. Many did not have clean water to drink. This caused outbreaks of diseases, such as cholera, in some parts of Iraq. For those who crossed into other countries, it was difficult to find jobs. And the living conditions were often terrible.

The United States tried to make life easier for displaced Iraqis. In 2007, it devoted $18 million to help resettle Iraqis. It also committed to greatly increasing the number of refugees that resettled within its borders. But much more support was needed to help rebuild the nation and resettle Iraqis.

But refugees often did not receive warm welcomes. They were viewed with suspicion by citizens and governments. People worried Iraqis would bring violence with them. Eventually, Jordan stopped allowing Iraqi men ages 18 to 35 from entering its borders. It thought this group of people might become violent. Syria also put restrictions on who could enter.

The United States resettled 13,726 Iraqis between October 1, 2006, and September 12, 2008.

US Troops Surge to Stabilize Region

The war in Iraq came to a crossroads in 2007. Fighting raged across the country. Iraqis questioned whether the new government was strong and inclusive enough to keep the country together. The coalition wanted to pull its troops out of Iraq. But it feared the Iraqi government would collapse without support. If it did, the country would face a brutal struggle for power between Sunnis, Shiites, and terrorist groups.

In January 2007, President Bush announced the United States would send 20,000 more soldiers to Iraq. Approximately 130,000 US soldiers were already in the country. Bush and military leaders from many countries also planned to partner with Iraqi communities to locate terrorists and control neighborhoods. The new plan became known as the Surge. Many Americans did not think the plan was a good idea. More than 3,000 US soldiers had already

Extremists take control of an Iraqi security forces vehicle in Mosul, Iraq.

The Council of Representatives of Iraq meets at the Baghdad Convention Center.

died in the war. But Bush and Iraqi Prime Minister al-Maliki went forward with the plan.

The number of US deaths in Iraq spiked in the first months of the Surge. But the effort got a big break in June 2007. Groups of Sunnis were paid to work with the US and Iraqi governments. Many of these groups formerly fought against the coalition. They now helped fight against terrorist groups.

The increased number of troops and changing alliances helped decrease violence in Iraq. But 899 US soldiers were killed. This was the most since the 2003 invasion. Still, violence dropped between Sunnis and Shiites. The government also showed signs of progress. Laws had kept many Sunnis from having government jobs. They were put in place to keep members of Hussein's government from retaking power. On January 12, 2008, the Iraqi government got rid of the laws. With an elected government, they were no longer needed. Still, US leaders warned the progress could be lost if coalition troops withdrew from Iraq too quickly. The region was still fairly unstable.

19

Number of US deaths in Iraq in May 2008, the fewest since the start of the war.

- Bush sent 20,000 more US soldiers to Iraq, starting in January 2007.
- In June 2007, Sunni groups started working with the Iraqi government to stop terrorists.
- In January 2008, the Iraqi government allowed Sunnis to return to government jobs.

US Forces Slowly Leave Iraq

Ramadi, the capital of the Anbar Province, was once the stronghold of the Sunni insurgency. But with growing Sunni support, the United States began pulling troops out of the region. On September 1, 2008, US leaders handed authority over to the Iraqi army and police. Two years before, Ramadi was the most deadly place in Iraq for US soldiers. Over time, the number of attacks dropped by 90 percent. Anbar was not the only place in Iraq where things were improving. It was the eleventh of 18 provinces to be handed over to Iraqi authorities.

In November 2008, Barack Obama was elected president of the United States. Many Americans were tired of the long war in Iraq. It had gone on for five years. And for the first time, Iraq appeared to be stable. During his presidency, Bush had put a plan in place for the United States to withdraw from Iraq. On November 17, the Iraqi government agreed to the timetable. US troops would leave Iraq by the end of 2011.

A parade in Ramadi marked the September 1 handover of power from US leaders to the Iraqi army and police.

4,500

Approximate number of US soldiers who died in the Iraq War.

- As violence decreased, the Iraqi government slowly took control of more of the country.
- US troops ended combat operations on August 31, 2010.
- The last US soldiers left Iraq on December 18, 2011.

VOTING AGAIN

In 2010, Iraqis went to the polls to vote once again. The parliament they elected was the most inclusive in the country's history. All the major political and ethnic groups were represented. In a very close vote, al-Maliki lost the role of prime minister to Ayad Allawi. But al-Maliki did not give up his office easily. After months of talks, the two men agreed to form a coalition government. Al-Maliki officially returned to the role of prime minister.

By June 30, 2009, US troops had pulled out of all Iraqi cities and towns. They put the Iraqi government in control. Across the nation, Iraqis celebrated. There was still tension over the Sunnis' lack of power in the government and a variety of other issues. But most Iraqis were happy that Iraqis once again controlled the country.

On August 31, 2010, US combat operations ended in Iraq. But Obama promised 50,000 soldiers would remain in Iraq until the end of 2011. They would train Iraqi security forces. On

December 18, 2011, the last US soldiers left Iraq. Iraq was working to become a democratic nation. But it still had a long way to go.

By June 30, 2009, all US troops had returned to their bases outside of cities and towns.

ISIS Gains Ground in the Middle East

After US troops left Iraq, tensions further increased between Sunnis and Shiites. It began when the government announced it would arrest Sunni Vice President Tariq al-Hashimi. Officials said he was linked to the deaths of Iraqi politicians. Sunnis saw the move as a way to decrease their influence in the government. Many protested and were attacked by government forces.

With Sunnis unhappy with the government, AQI saw a chance to grow its power. It recruited in Sunni areas, such as the Anbar Province. Soon, AQI changed its name to the Islamic State of Iraq and Syria (ISIS). Many Sunnis did not share ISIS's extreme plans for the government. But they were upset with the Iraqi government. More Sunnis began to fight for ISIS. The group took control of the Anbar Province. And

in 2014, ISIS captured new territory. This included Iraq's second-largest city, Mosul. Haider al-Abadi was appointed as prime minister of Iraq in 2014. He worked to build a government in which Sunnis felt more included. He wanted to gain unity in order to fight against ISIS.

In September 2014, Obama said the United States would support

AL-QAEDA AND ISIS

Both Al-Qaeda and ISIS share the goal of creating a single Islamic State. Al-Qaeda views this as a long-term goal. But ISIS wants to reach this goal now. Al-Qaeda and ISIS are viewed as competitors. And they often disagree about strategies.

20,000
Number of non-Iraqi people believed to have joined ISIS.

- The Iraqi government announced it would arrest the Sunni vice president.
- Violence resumed between Sunnis and Shiites.
- ISIS recruited Sunnis who were not happy with the government.
- The United States sent air attacks to fight ISIS, which slowed the group's progress in Iraq.
- ISIS spread to other parts of the Middle East.

the Iraqi government in the fight against ISIS. US air strikes slowed the spread of ISIS in Iraq in 2014 and 2015. But the group kept gaining influence in the Middle East. Supported by governments around the world, Iraqi troops were still fighting to regain control of the country as of 2015.

On November 13, 2015, ISIS staged a series of attacks on Paris, France, killing more than 100 people.

12 Key Dates

January 17, 1991
The United States begins Operation Desert Storm.

September 11, 2001
Al-Qaeda terrorists hijack four US planes and use them as weapons.

October 7, 2001
The United States begins Operation Enduring Freedom in Afghanistan.

March 19, 2003
The United States turns its focus to the war in Iraq.

April 28, 2004
Photos of prisoner abuse at Abu Ghraib appear on US television.

October 6, 2004
The Iraq Survey Group releases a report saying there are no weapons of mass destruction in Iraq.

January 30, 2005
Iraqis vote in the country's first free elections in more than 50 years.

October 15, 2005
Iraqis approve the country's new constitution.

February 22, 2006
An AQI attack on a Shiite mosque triggers a rise in fighting between Sunnis and Shiites.

January 12, 2008
The Iraqi government gets rid of laws keeping Sunnis from working in the government.

August 31, 2010
US combat operations end in Iraq.

December 18, 2011
All US troops exit Iraq.

Glossary

coalition
A group of allies working for a common goal.

drone
An aircraft that operates through remote control.

Geneva Conventions
Laws outlining how prisoners of war, wounded soldiers, and civilians should be treated during times of war.

hijacked
Taken over by force.

insurgent
A rebel or revolutionary.

oppression
A state of being unjustly controlled.

referendum
A vote that addresses one particular issue.

refugees
People who are forced to leave their country.

terrorism
The use of violence or threats of violence for a political goal.

weapons of mass destruction
Nuclear, chemical, or biological weapons that can injure or kill large numbers of people.

For More Information

Books

Challen, Paul C. *Surviving 9/11*. New York: Rosen Publishing, 2016.

Summers, Elizabeth. *Weapons and Vehicles of the Iraq War*. North Mankato, MN: Capstone Press, 2016.

Winter, Max. *The Afghanistan War*. Mankato, MN: Child's World, 2015.

Visit 12StoryLibrary.com

Scan the code or use your school's login at **12StoryLibrary.com** for recent updates about this topic and a full digital version of this book. Enjoy free access to:

- Digital ebook
- Breaking news updates
- Live content feeds
- Videos, interactive maps, and graphics
- Additional web resources

Note to educators: Visit 12StoryLibrary.com/register to sign up for free premium website access. Enjoy live content plus a full digital version of every 12-Story Library book you own for every student at your school.

Index

About the Author

Jon Westmark is a writer and editor living in Minneapolis, Minnesota. When he is not working with words, Westmark enjoys rock climbing, watching football, and playing the cello.

READ MORE FROM 12-STORY LIBRARY

Every 12-Story Library book is available in many formats. For more information, visit 12StoryLibrary.com.